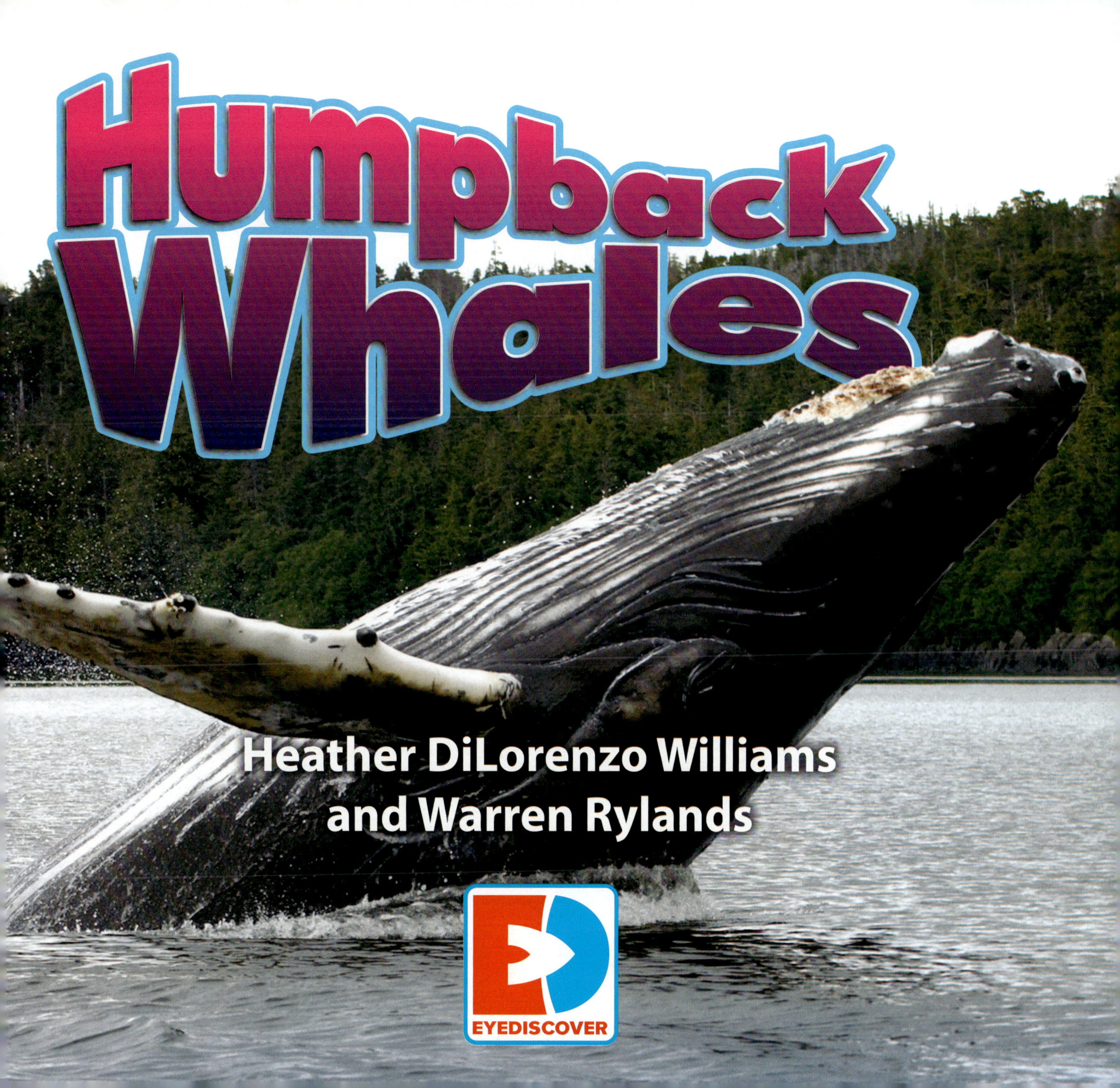

# Humpback Whales

Heather DiLorenzo Williams
and Warren Rylands

EYEDISCOVER

Go to **www.eyediscover.com** and enter this book's unique code.

**BOOK CODE**

**AVB59623**

**EYEDISCOVER** brings you optic readalongs that support active learning.

Published by $AV^2$ by Weigl
350 5th Avenue, 59th Floor New York, NY 10118
Website: www.eyediscover.com



Library of Congress Control Number: 2018953510

ISBN 978-1-4896-8159-1 (hardcover)

Printed in the United States of America
in Brainerd, Minnesota
1 2 3 4 5 6 7 8 9 0 22 21 20 19 18

082018
120917

Project Coordinator: John Willis
Designer: Mandy Christiansen

Weigl acknowledges Alamy, Getty Images, iStock, and Shutterstock as the primary image suppliers for this title.

EYEDISCOVER provides enriched content, optimized for tablet use, that supplements and complements this book. EYEDISCOVER books strive to create inspired learning and engage young minds in a total learning experience.

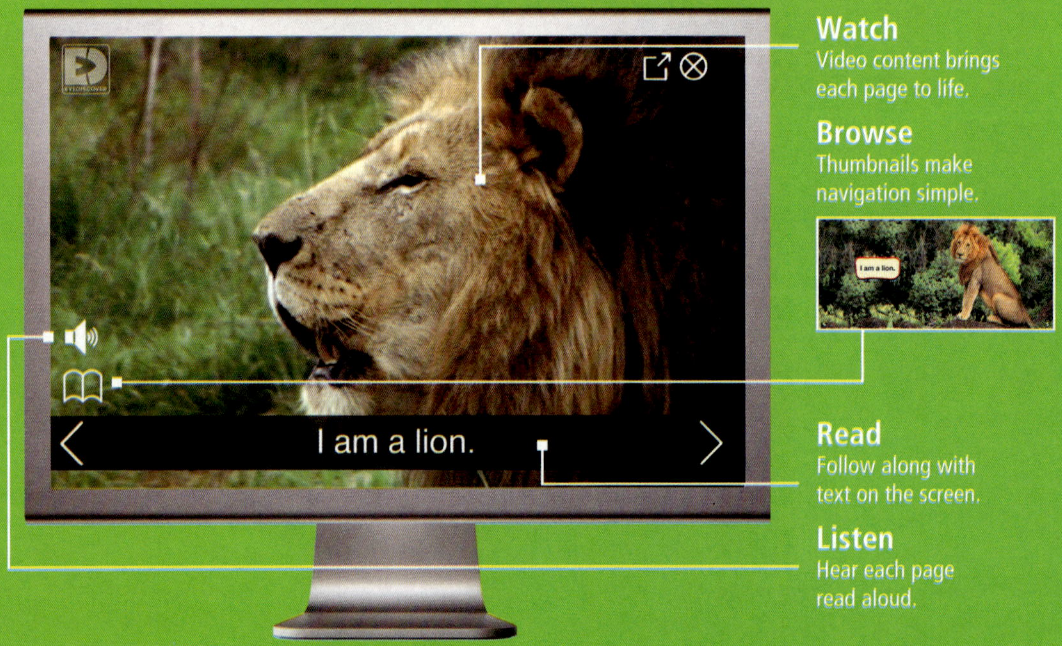


## Your EYEDISCOVER Optic Readalongs come alive with...

**Audio**
Listen to the entire book read aloud.

**Video**
High resolution videos turn each spread into an optic readalong.

**OPTIMIZED FOR**
- TABLETS
- WHITEBOARDS
- COMPUTERS
- AND MUCH MORE!

# Humpback Whales

In this book, you will learn about

- how they look
- where they live
- what they do

and much more!

Humpback whales are large animals. They live in oceans.

Some humpbacks live near Alaska in the summer. They move to warmer waters near Hawai'i in the winter.

Humpback whales get their name from the shape their backs make when they dive.

Humpbacks often jump out of the water. This is called breaching.

They live in groups called pods. Pods are often two or three whales but can be much larger.

Humpback whales talk to each other by singing. These songs can be heard from far away.

Humpbacks whales eat fish and tiny shrimp called krill.

Baby humpback whales are called calves. They are born knowing how to swim.

Many people like watching humpback whales jump out of the water. It is important for people to watch from a safe distance.

# HUMPBACK WHALES BY THE NUMBERS

Humpback whales can weigh up **40 tons**. That is the same weight as **20 cars**. (36 metric tons)

**Humpback whales** can hold their breath under water up to **45 minutes**.

A humpback whale's song can be **20 minutes** long.

**Humpback whales** travel about **6,000 miles** a year. (9,656 km)

There are about **40,000** humpback whales in the ocean today.

**Female** humpback whales are about **50 feet** long. **Male** whales are smaller.

(15 meters)

# KEY WORDS

Research has shown that as much as 65 percent of all written material published in English is made up of 300 words. These 300 words cannot be taught using pictures or learned by sounding them out. They must be recognized by sight. This book contains 48 common sight words to help young readers improve their reading fluency and comprehension. This book also teaches young readers several important content words, such as proper nouns. These words are paired with pictures to aid in learning and improve understanding.

| Page | Sight Words First Appearance |
|---|---|
| 4 | animals, are, in, large, live, they |
| 7 | move, near, some, the, to |
| 8 | from, get, make, name, their, when |
| 11 | is, of, often, out, this, water |
| 12 | be, but, can, much, or, three, two |
| 15 | away, by, each, far, other, talk, these |
| 16 | and, eat |
| 19 | how |
| 20 | a, for, important, it, like, many, people, watch |

| Page | Content Words First Appearance |
|---|---|
| 4 | humpback whales, oceans |
| 7 | Alaska, Hawai'i, summer, waters, winter |
| 8 | backs, dive |
| 11 | breaching |
| 12 | groups, pods |
| 15 | singing, songs |
| 16 | fish, krill, shrimp |
| 19 | calves |

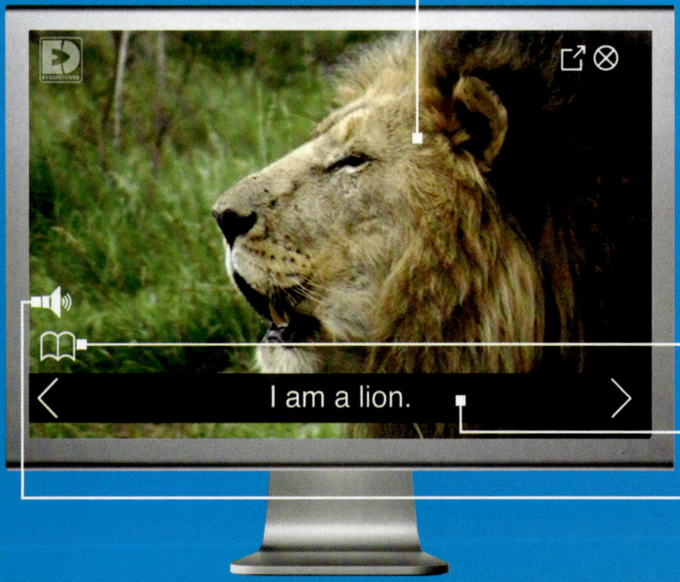


**Watch**
Video content brings each page to life.

**Browse**
Thumbnails make navigation simple.

**Read**
Follow along with text on the screen.

**Listen**
Hear each page read aloud.

EYEDISCOVER

**Go to www.eyediscover.com and enter this book's unique code.**

**BOOK CODE**

**AVB59623**